Survivalism for Hedonists

Survivalism for Hedonists
Dylan McNulty-Holmes

QUERENCIA

Querencia Press
Chicago Illinois

QUERENCIA PRESS

© Copyright 2023

Dylan McNulty-Holmes

All Rights Reserved

No reproduction, copy or transmission of this publication may be made without written permission.
No paragraph of this publication may be reproduced, copied or transmitted save with the written permission of the author.

Any person who commits any unauthorized act in relation to this publication may be liable to criminal prosecution and civil claims for damages.

ISBN 978 1 959118 54 1

www.querenciapress.com

First Published in 2023

Querencia Press

Chicago IL

Printed & Bound in the United States of America

CONTENTS

Macarons for Tourists 9
The King of a Rainy Country 10
A Handful of Dirt 11
Protoromance 12
A Lover's Oasis 13
Killers 14
Survivalism for Hedonists 15
Glossy Monsters 16
As Ruly as a Body Can Be 17
Brazen 18
Front Room Blues 19
Dinner, Reservations 20
Breaking in at Least Four Places 21
Glaciers and Sickles 22
The Bridesmaid 23
Lockdown, Denial 24
A Blessing for Transition 25
Masc for Femme 26
My Year as a Practicing Queer 27
Nyctinasty 29
Ordinary Talk 30
Hothouse Lovesong 32

Afterword 35
Acknowledgements 38

Macarons for Tourists

Passionsfrucht-Haselnuss, Tonka:
I'll need concrete steps at some point, but now
the seatbelt light goes on and Berlin rises up to greet us,
established by its fungal smell
and the way it metamorphoses my doubt into guilt—
it's all practice in the inner workings
of alleyways, eventually.

Walnuss-Holunder, Kokos:
How grand, you own a whole language in my head.
I cross my arms tight against my chest,
against bitter cold, tendrils of your hair,
public littering, small birds and fallen petals.

Mandarine-Minze, Earlgrey:
Cast a blanket over me, gently suffuse me—
Tell me that outliers aren't prophecies,
that crying might eject this pain—
if I'll listen, beat out a new song for me
against the taxi window.

The King of a Rainy Country

I can use this
        fire in the hole
To box in, push out
        anyone who dares
        stretch towards—

As if you were still here,
        particularly fond of
Making objectively undesirable
        the thought
Of slowly French kissing
        him—

Essentially fiction,
        my investment in the
        we could've left together—

Given up on dreams of a home we could keep.
This spectacle is trying to tear out of my body,
        and I need a fistful, flying,
        falling for something—falling in love.

A Handful of Dirt

to each soft bed, Rain.	The bitterest
sort of music. I would love, rooted but expansive,
acknowledging:	This is why I was.

The only way I can
paint this: without definition,
        movements.

It's hard for me to understand this particular
fucking with abandon, the soft temperature
of this emptiness and The Perks of Being
pinched. Prior to this appropriation, I'd been
intricate lines in wood and minerals—
been pushed against the wall,
meant nothing—

I had been nights so cold
        your bed feels like driftwood in the arctic.

Protoromance

Look, I'm flying!

Spied glimpses of fondness,
sang Happy Birthday,
stole money, got money back.

Desolation   left you at the airport,
Assumed my role,   left no room
For skin,   roses; after eight,
the element   of surprise;

walked calmly through my childhood.

A Lover's Oasis

Sediment of solitude.

A sea of poised, experienced dancers
craft answers, ask for better influences
make co-conspirators. With only a slight
sadness   I rub myself against them.

How these temples talk
            through kisses landing on whatever part
            I can get my hands on building
            bathing the whole room in noise
letting them lick   and grasp   and bite
                                    resigned
                                    to this
            Sediment of solitude.

Still there is talk at the bar,
            fires to be fought—

I have been here two months now,
            kicking myself in spite,
            but throwing myself right back
into the amusement park, to this spree of brilliant lies;

I want to step fully inside each thought   and never care
                about the heavy hands of strangers.

Killers

I was
clashing colours on the walls.
I searched for
some disturbance miles below—sound? swarm? crowd?

These are the watercolours she made,
a hastily dispatched scotch,
skinny jeans the boys are so fond of,
fit into   used pieces—

These are the watercolours she made,
sat on the banks,
lost—   those sweethearts
of evening—   Dear God, please let her be okay.

Where was she the night
          under, warm—
Put to good use
          without looking—

Survivalism for Hedonists

This dusty-windowed, battered-taxi performance of happiness
only hails our doubts; reminds us of our hardships,
the absurdities of our plight;

why couldn't they just leave us alone,
        murmur among themselves?

The price: we paid   did not
        enjoy   were not seduced   now
cannot be left, are always followed
can never   quite   move   towards—

Can this be finished by thumbs
clumsily punching numbers?
I just want to get thoughtless   to capsize,
to double-expose the film,   overlay the memory
with softcore porn,   to strand   myself
between   senseless gorging   and impossible dreams
of sunlight,
        again.

A bloody-minded calm; a calm borne of submission;
assuming all responsibility; closing the door, locking it;
withering; inhaling sharply; running out
of meaning.

Glossy Monsters

I wanted to believe: if I just went along with it,
the blood
would disappear—

Quickly,
the anti-us vigilante patrol is headed straight
this way—

It's all very well and good to acknowledge I need
to relax, lay it all out
onto canvas, turpentine, rusted metal,
find use for confidential tones and gestures—

The day often begins
the time we need it most, with the bravery
of the ever again—

Picture
me, keeping my head down, pushing through—
crying until I'm emptied out, until

Drowsiness coats me in
remembrance:
the party, Thursday night,
that perfume I like, these
stale
re-edits,
how I could once
name the blood
an old favourite—

Come back to the flat.
Is beauty's new face
gone?

When it hits
this time
I won't
humour
high school
endings.

As Ruly as a Body Can Be

Ah, I've got sorrier tales to tell—
things bitter-lacquered,
more poetic—but
they turn me wordless,
my objections
settling in my glass, cooling.

Sadness recognising itself—particularly cruel,
these vapours of possibility, now
the night begins to paint us sober—but
here we are, still able to sing with hearts
and gusts, to render window sockets
glassless.

Our flirtation,
loose teeth in bad dreams—
humbly, you inhale
the kiss of perfume I tenderly dabbed
on this still, grey morning,
hoping today, you would find it here.

Brazen

gouged and dismembered centuries here trembling
together as she's laying on top of me, or else
is healing old wounds, comfortably fitting in
the Hellos we thought we alone   had totemised.

was proud. in the end. was lucky. encouraged my dreams right
in of the corner of my vision, telling a higher power:
this is only theatre, where everything is wheeled
and the streets are more carpeted in petals.

taste through familiar bodily dives
All Those Years of worrying about how hard it was
upon the earth, but:
Better Dead Than A Coward.

Front Room Blues

Oh chilling doubt:
I'm never so interested
in proffering a drag, or letting you take it.
Each screaming teakettle arrives
into evening, coloured lights from the TV
thump against windows. We were miles
that day, but hope
is a moron—
whole sheaths of
paper still rip,
vans still rattle,
this strength still
eliminates poetry.

Dinner, Reservations

In oil, in spice:
  I was once the second-rate singer
  whose songs   scarcely   mattered,
  matter.

My smile changes to something clandestine,
  antithesis, synthesis:

The way home smells of fried garlic,
  making me want something I can squeeze
  out of this:

I just snuck out of this whole week,
  had a nosebleed:

The Goddess Who Created this Passing Magic
  was not trying to limit us— she sees the love
  I wish   I could squeeze out:

I just snuck out of movement, the fountain,
  out of friends' lives: out of this singular piece
  of mind.

Breaking in at Least Four Places

Stand up.

Can you name what
chaos made me, the good
recorded, kept? I'm glad for the
terrible, those sharp yelps of suffering—

He was
driving home from the hospital with her baby—breathless
      outside
            me, this throbbing vein.

Glaciers and Sickles

In truth:
We do, I say—and what I mean is, I hope we can
When we're missing the sweetest parts
Of what could be
In the contests, the scything,
The business of melting, disambiguating
As all of me disappears into her:
Velvet sweater, satin bomber, thoughts.

I disown my mother on an ordinary
Sunday, 31st January, 2021, with a hurt
Never just for myself—for everyone
Whose neck has snapped and twisted
In living rigor mortis,
Who's had to learn the difference
Between bravery and recklessness,
Who's said goodbye
        for now   at least

The Bridesmaid

I need to get to the point
in the night where
the water will release me

The women, serendipitous,
the friction, caught kisses
intended to be hopeful, or kind

The gender indeterminate protagonist has crossed the seas
in garish shorts, has been confronted,
is now dressed in a wedding gown, is furious

The outer surface of the storm
greets my mouth, a mouth
who is hidden or trying to be free

I wish I had looked, could actually have seen,
this work we hook upon each other; that how I do this job
is none of your fucking business

But I truly wanted
a blessing for this wedding,
in remembrance of time flown—

But got a plunge, a diving board,
an ending to the story I've told about this skin,
the thing I want to build here.
Got what hurts.

Lockdown, Denial

The Fool explores, towheaded
he asked, and was trained
in ritual male sacrifice,
which he cloaked in the tang of sweat
and vodka.

Hythloday, the nonsense peddler,
tells himself this thread
he retraces might just be
the product of storms
or histrionics; second guesses,
wonders if a worse heartache
is on the horizon.

But I was halfway here before then anyway:
cold to nights in fishnets,
spurious omens. I asked, and was given
this lovely death, piling into
every sensation trauma engenders;
all the different ways
we are tricksters unto ourselves
when openness is taken away.

A Blessing for Transition

Whisper
In pursuit   of some truth
No matter what it is—

As ancient cultures
Sacrificed   kings
We will claim this planet as our own,
Press quarrelling mouths   close

To be   reborn of crops,
Through sacrifice
Of deadly   watchful   cult
Of pink keys   and blue keys

The way to be a dream   after so many years
Cry,   flood back in glimpses,   slivers of lightning
Under all the moons we have yet to worship—

Tell me what you asked for,
Sent up   thought   would never get
Your deafest parts   your heart   red
Red, the colour   of self   you try to ignore
The part   inadvertently spilled
So much easier   than predictable   laborious
never, ever, ever—

Let wild herbs silver you   prophet   reconfigure
without biography   without history
may these hours   promise you   something—or,
better yet,   show it.

Masc for Femme

It's a lot, this wanting
to keep sweetnesses, to exist outside
of conservative status quo bedrock—
to be loved, respected, and desired—
Devil Moon, I have no idea
about feel-good, or making-the-most, or bra-sizes—

But these sparks rise out of the ground—
climaxes, anti-climaxes, the glory of
delicate silver chains, loud brassy fake jewels,
deviant afterlives, mysterious treasures,
slugs with bold black etchings against pavements—
a glossary of resistances.   There's something
lost, singing—

The Devil Moon
presses her fingers deep into my dimples,
making me forget sweaters, curse love terms
embedded into me like chunks of terracotta—
works me over, leaves me dressed
in flowers, sprayed across my chest.

My Year as a Practicing Queer

I once had such a succinct
and lovely nose for reason.
If this is goodbye, please know
it's absolutely in spite of myself:
my saliva-wet fingertips,
relief, turned on, at last,
on my own terms. It's easier
to retreat than it is to go slow,
but finally: the fullness of this
spills over words.

Running on a streak
of claiming my territory,
celebrating the difference:
killing that old jumble
of silk scarves, legs bent back;
promises, assumptions,
never caring to ask.

Remembered mornings
stretching into sunlight,
sense of impatience for
5am with a beautiful girl
on my arm—but I loved
to forget, keep them
as strangers, dream into
the coloured lights
at the party after—

Told myself: blot out their face,
stop imagining next
we meet, stop checking
the restraints, relate it all
back to destruction, stop
bracing for escape—

Did not count on eyes
that reciprocate; getting stuck in bed
with a desperately wanted someone;
my skin, forgetting all
those ersatz versions
of myself, feeling
something new.

Nyctinasty

She tucks her coinages
Into late afternoons, cooking, thinking:
Someone has to
Bite down.   Will I be cleaved neatly?

Will this hint of ostentation
Swarm into black smoke? Will she be first
To lick my armpits and feet, cover me in glitter?
Will this hint of ostentation
Signal my insecurity, incite me to,
Almost certainly, die?
Will I be sharp, a whiplash?
Will I save all the plants? Have I somewhere to be?

Answer: I am loved
at the pace of real life.   Preserve
this darkness that falls around
us—   How many
burials, into chests, into pillows—
I must have been asleep for many hundreds of seconds
to have noticed:
When I turned away from you
Towards my plastic cup of wine
I
          petalled

Ordinary Talk

Writing as investigation: how disabled bodies mark us out,
but invite us into dreams of different futures.

Dreaming that feels like foraging,
like an occupation.

This year has been tiresome, overlaid with struggle,
pain singing right through it.

If yelling is an inquiry into the resentments of others,
afterwards: how long must we rest?

Is it death to accept exasperation,
to run on a streak of take take take?

Working on poems, which neighbour the
all is well. alles ist gut.

Writing as learning how to open, to love so fiercely,
to understand the *all is well. alles ist gut:*

>(1) to pay in carelessness; to capsize;
>(2) to push prams, use fancy moisturisers; to be spritzed with pleasure;
>(3) actions modifying clamouring egos; to sleep in a bed assured of one's work;
>(4) to be competent in the challenges of this time;
>to struggle;
>(5) open up, open to me; tell yourself you can, then recognise me; let us spin together in the cool water;

fear fogs my thoughts
but I shan't forget the drop of anguish,
the blood, the mask thrown down,
the angers I try to somehow unfeel
in the back of my throat.

Hothouse Lovesong

Lavish, in every possible configuration;
in pockets, on eyelashes;

Work will feel   like a different city;

Others will acknowledge   this body's magnificence.
Nobody will be vexed   this airless Sunday
Will sweep upward from the streets,
   rising,
        daylighting, windows
                    will burn,
today
will take into account every
        inherited blister—
Survive nightmares, wake up
        young, smell
        like curiosity—
                commit
        itself
to transgression.

Afterword

These poems began as cut-ups from the notebooks I have kept consistently for the past nine years. I used a very simple Python script to randomise page and line locations in each notebook, then selected words from each of those lines to form a first draft of a poem. Each poem represents one notebook I kept between 2014 and 2021.

Using this method means I was not just exploding and rearranging my own words, but the words of many, many artists whose work I have admired over the past nine years. Where a quotation of more than five words was used, I have credited them in the Acknowledgements. There are numerous sources from which I've borrowed only a word or two, but without whom, this collection would not exist. So, thank you to the following found text sources, in order of appearance:

"Today I'm Yours" by Mary Gaitskill

"Mean Free Path" by Ben Lerner

"The Hours" by Michael Cunningham

"The Perks of Being a Wallflower" (the title of), by Stephen Chbosky

"Blog Hop: A Writing Q&A" by Erica Eller

"Birdman" by Rachel McCrum

"$28.40" by Siobhan Bledsoe

"INTENTINTERRUPTIONS" by Sampurna Chattarji

"Instant Art" (the program of), an exhibition at The Impossible Project Lab

"The Bloody Chamber" (the title of), by Angela Carter

"The Goddess Experience" by Gisèle Scanlon

"Those Who Leave and Those Who Stay" by Elena Ferrante

"isamaya ffrench asks what would jeanne-salomé rochat do?" by Isamaya Ffrench

"Beauty Papers" (the blurb of), edited by Maxine Leonard and Valerie Wickes

"Better Dead Than a Coward" (the title of), by Laura Davis

"Soon I Will Be Dead and My Bones Will Be Free to Wreak Havoc Upon the Earth Once More" (the title of), by Sean Morley

"Say Hello to Your New Step Mummy" (the title of), by Lou Sanders

"Can a Famous Actor & 3 Nightlife Experts Really Open a New Dive Bar?" (the title of), by Robert Simonson

"Somehow I Became Respectable" by John Waters

"Aurora" by Eileen Myles

"Reborn: Journals and Notebooks, 1947-1963" by Susan Sontag

"Experiments" by Bernadette Mayer

"Design Matters" (the title of), by Debbie Millman

"Rules of Life" by Valerie Vale

"Stand-Up for Her" (the title of), by Bridget Christie

"Saunas to sourdough: Unesco updates culture heritage list" by Angela Guiffrida

"3 Women" (the title of), directed by Robert Altman

"Who Is the Boy and Who Is the Girl?" by Marisa Crane

"A Blessing for a Wedding" by Jane Hirschfield

"Blue Mythologies" by Carol Mavor

"Like Others" by Jane Hirschfield

"The Art of Fiction, No. 245: George Saunders" by Benjamin Nugent

"Mabon the Sacred King and Sacrifice" by Blue Star Owl

"Upon Realising Golden Girls Was Coming to an End" by Daniel Lavery

"FLAPPERHOUSE- Year Five" (the blurb of), edited by Joseph P. O'Brien

"Ordinary People" by Diana Evans

"Masculinities: Liberation Through Photography" (the program of), an exhibition at Gropius Bau

"Too Lost in You" by Dianne Warren, performed by The Sugababes

"Kalanchoe Daigremonita" by Juliette Patissier

"Local Girl" by Neko Case

"The Killing of a Sacred Deer" (the title of), directed by Yorgos Lanthimos

"At Berlin Schönefeld Airport" by Marília Garcia

"Lithograph (1955)" by Martha Sprackland

"Prep School Confidential: Lexi Freiman's novel of teens, cyborgs, and critical theory" by Andrea Long Chu

"How Do We Write Now?" by Patricia Lockwood

"The Body is Not an Apology" by Sonya Renee Taylor

The Wikipedia entry for "Robert Angermann"

"In the End, It Was All About Love" by Musa Okwonga

"Craft Chaps" by Chen Chen

The Wikipedia page for "Daylighting"

Acknowledgements

"Macarons for Tourists" borrows three macaron flavours from the menu of Art Sucré patisserie in Berlin.

"The King of a Rainy Country" first appeared in "Love Letter to a Thousand Yesterdays" by Sunday Mornings at the River Press. It is named after a novel by Brigid Brophy. The line "given up on dreams of a home we could keep" is paraphrased from "Holiday" by Julie Byrne (from "Rooms With Walls and Windows," Orindal Records, 2014).

"A Lover's Oasis" first a appeared in "Love Letter to a Thousand Yesterdays" by Sunday Mornings at the River Press. It is named after a lyric from "Tea for Two" by Vincent Youmans and Irving Caesar.

"Killers" is named after a short story by Susan Steinberg. The line "these are the watercolours she made" is borrowed from "dear hairless erin" by Sara June Woods (from "~yr various hairlessnesses~," self-published, 2015).

"As Ruly as a Body Can Be" first a appeared in "Love Letter to a Thousand Yesterdays" by Sunday Mornings at the River Press.

"Dinner, Reservations" borrows the line "the goddess who created this passing" from "The Goddess Who Created This Passing World" by Alice Notley (from "Selected Poems," Talisman House, 1993).

"Glaciers and Sickles" borrows the line "disambiguation [...] all of him disappears into her" from "Scallop" by J.L. Akagi (Strange Horizons, 2020).

"The Bridesmaid" borrows the lines "the outer surface of the storm" and "who is hidden or trying to be free" from "How to Write an Autobiographical Novel" by Alexander Chee (Bloomsbury Publishing, 2018).

"Masc for Femme" first appeared in ANMLY.

"Nyctinasty" first appeared in miniskirt magazine.

"Ordinary Talk" first appeared in ANMLY. It is named after a song by Half Waif. The line "I shall forget the drop of anguish" is paraphrased from "I shall know why – when time is over" by Emily Dickinson (as quoted in "The Summer Without Men" by Siri Hustvedt, Macmillan, 2011). The line "all is well. alles ist gut." is borrowed from an advert for Malimo.

"Hothouse Lovesong" paraphrases the line "swept upward from the streets like rising" from "An American Childhood" by Annie Dillard (as it appears in "An Annie Dillard Reader," HarperCollins, 2009).